P9-BVH-486

MEI SHENG ON HIS CLIMBING PERCH.

HUA MEI IS READY FOR LUNCH.

IT'S A LONG WAY DOWN, MEI SHENG!

PEEKABOO, MEI SHENG!

PANDA MATH

LEARNING ABOUT SUBTRACTION
FROM HUA MEI AND MEI SHENG

BY ANN WHITEHEAD NAGDA

IN COLLABORATION WITH THE SAN DIEGO ZOO

Henry Holt and Company

New York

JUNIOR ROOM
LUDINGTON PUBLIC LIBRARY
BRYN MAWR, PA 19010

A TEENY TINY BABY

AT FIVE DAYS OLD MEI SHENG DOESN'T
LOOK MUCH LIKE A PANDA YET.

THE PANDA'S WEIGHT

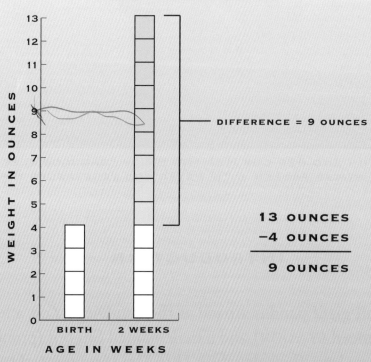

DIFFERENCE = 9 OUNCES

13 OUNCES
−4 OUNCES
———————
9 OUNCES

Subtraction means finding the **difference** between two numbers. When Mei Sheng was born, he weighed about 4 ounces. He was the size and weight of one stick of butter. Two weeks later, he was much bigger—he weighed 13 ounces. The graph above shows his weight at both times. Each block represents one ounce. You can see that the difference between Mei Sheng's weight at birth and his weight at two weeks is 9 ounces.

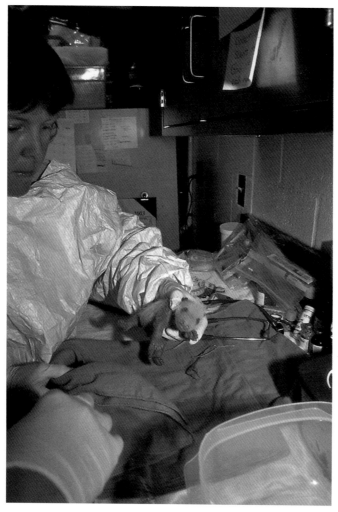

DR. MEG SUTHERLAND-SMITH, A ZOO VETERINARIAN,
EXAMINES MEI SHENG WHEN HE'S TWO WEEKS OLD.

One summer afternoon a giant panda named Bai Yun gave birth to a male cub. Cameras placed in the birthing den allowed the San Diego Zoo staff to watch the mother panda and her newborn cub without disturbing them. Mei Sheng, as the cub was later named, was so tiny at first that observers had trouble seeing him on the TV monitors. Instead they listened for his loud cry. Bai Yun cuddled the fragile infant against her chest with one massive arm. The newborn cub had sparse white fur all over his body, and his eyes were closed. He looked more like a rat than a giant panda.

BAMBOO AT THE ZOO

AT THREE WEEKS OLD HUA MEI IS
STILL TOO YOUNG TO EAT BAMBOO.

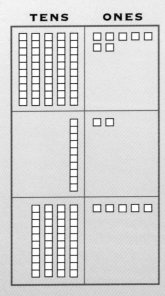

TENS   ONES

57 BAMBOO SPECIES
AT THE ZOO

−12 BAMBOO SPECIES
EATEN BY PANDAS

45 BAMBOO SPECIES
NOT EATEN BY PANDAS

Wild pandas usually eat only bamboo. Two thousand species, or kinds, of bamboo grow around the world. There are 57 species in the San Diego Zoo and at their Wild Animal Park. Some species grow along paths and in exhibits, but others are used to feed animals. The pandas at the Zoo eat 12 different kinds of bamboo. How many kinds are not eaten by pandas?

In the **decimal** or **base 10** system, numbers are grouped by tens. In the chart above, the number 57 is written as 5 groups of ten and 7 ones. The number 12 is written as 1 ten and 2 ones. To subtract, take 2 ones away from 7 ones, which is 5 ones. Then take 1 ten away from 5 tens, which is 4 tens. The difference between 57 and 12 is 45. So 45 species of bamboo are not eaten by pandas.

MEI SHENG SQUAWKS FOR HIS MOTHER WHEN HE'S ONE MONTH OLD.

Panda mothers stay with their cubs almost continuously throughout the first month. During this time the mothers usually don't eat anything. Bai Yun waited until Mei Sheng was three days old before she left the den to get a drink of water. She had waited until the fifth day to leave Hua Mei, her first cub.

The panda mom seemed less protective of her second cub. She didn't hold him all the time as she did with her first baby, and she left him more often. Still, she was a caring and attentive mother. If the cub squawked while Bai Yun was out of the den, she would rush back in, gently pick up the baby in her mouth, and cuddle him in her arms until he fell asleep again.

IT'S ALWAYS LUNCHTIME

WHILE BAI YUN IS OUTSIDE THE DEN EATING BAMBOO,
DR. LEE YOUNG EXAMINES SIX-WEEK-OLD MEI SHENG.

TENS	ONES	
		14 HOURS
		−6 HOURS
		8 HOURS

Wild pandas spend 14 hours each day eating bamboo. In the Zoo, pandas eat for only 6 hours a day. To find out how much less time a panda in the Zoo spends eating, subtract 6 from 14.

First, figure out what you need to subtract from 14 to get 10, which is a "friendly" number because it's an easy number to subtract from anything. Subtract 4 of the 6 hours from 14 to get 10.

14 − 4 = 10 (SUBTRACT 4 ONES TO GET 10)

You've taken one part away. Then subtract 2, the other part of the 6 hours, to get 8.

10 − 2 = 8 (THEN SUBTRACT 2 ONES)

So pandas in the Zoo spend 8 fewer hours a day eating bamboo than pandas in the wild.

SENIOR KEEPER KATHY HAWK HOLDS MEI SHENG AT SEVEN WEEKS.

Once panda cubs are two months old, they begin to scoot around the den. Their mothers spend more time away from the den eating bamboo. The first time Hua Mei wriggled out of the den, Bai Yun took her right back inside. With Mei Sheng, the mother panda was more relaxed and even carried her cub outside into the garden area. And she didn't respond to his every little squawk like she did with Hua Mei.

When Mei Sheng was really distressed, though, his mother would come and comfort him with little pats. Bai Yun licked her cub frequently, cleaning the milk off his mouth after he'd nursed and eating his waste to keep the den clean. In the wild, the smell of milk or poop in the den could attract a predator.

HUNGRY, HUNGRY PANDA

On a typical day, Bai Yun's keepers might offer her 41 pounds of bamboo, and she might eat all but 12 pounds. By subtracting how much is left from how much bamboo was offered to her, you can figure out how much she ate.

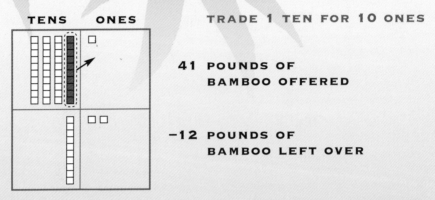

TENS   ONES

TRADE 1 TEN FOR 10 ONES

**41 POUNDS OF
BAMBOO OFFERED**

**−12 POUNDS OF
BAMBOO LEFT OVER**

Since 2 is more than 1, you need to **regroup** the numbers so that you have enough ones to do the subtraction. In the first chart above, the number 41 is shown as 4 tens and 1 one. If you trade a ten for 10 ones, or regroup the number, then you have 3 tens remaining. Add the 10 ones you traded to the 1 one for a total of 11 ones.

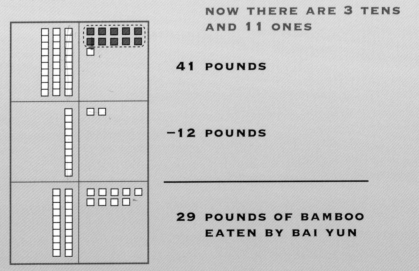

**NOW THERE ARE 3 TENS
AND 11 ONES**

41 POUNDS

−12 POUNDS

**29 POUNDS OF BAMBOO
EATEN BY BAI YUN**

Now you can subtract 2 ones from 11 ones to get 9. Next subtract 1 ten from 3 tens to get 2 tens. The difference is 29. Bai Yun ate 29 pounds of bamboo.

MEI SHENG TAKES HIS FIRST WOBBLY STEPS.

At the age of three months, a baby panda begins to sit up and can move around the den more easily. The first time Hua Mei sat up, she wiggled her front feet and then toppled over. Mei Sheng took his first wobbly steps at the same age, and he even managed to walk out of the den on his own. He also began biting and patting his mother playfully.

By this time Bai Yun was back to eating her normal portion of bamboo every day. Sometimes she brought bamboo into the den to eat. Bamboo grown at the Zoo provided about 75 percent of her diet. Bai Yun also ate carrots, yams, and high-fiber biscuits, which look like dog biscuits. Her favorite treat was an apple.

WILD PANDA, ZOO PANDA

GAO GAO WAS HESITANT ABOUT CLIMBING TREES, SO HIS KEEPERS HID TREATS IN BRANCHES TO ENCOURAGE HIM.

Mei Sheng's parents were both 11 years old when he was born. A wild panda lives for about 15 years. But zoo pandas can live for 30 years. To find out how much longer Bai Yun and Gao Gao might live, subtract 11 years, their age at Mei Sheng's birth, from 30 years, the age they might reach.

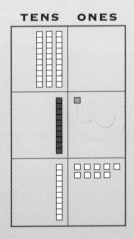

TENS ONES

30 YEARS (ESTIMATED LIFE SPAN)

−11 YEARS (AGE AT MEI SHENG'S BIRTH)

19 YEARS (ESTIMATED YEARS REMAINING)

You could use regrouping to solve this problem. Another way is to subtract each **place value.** In the chart above, the number 30 is shown as 3 tens and no ones, and 11 is shown as 1 ten and 1 one. Start with the tens and subtract 10 from 30, which is 20.

30 − 10 = 20 (SUBTRACT THE TENS)

Then count back from 20 by 1 to get 19.

20 − 1 = 19 (THEN SUBTRACT THE ONES)

So the difference between 30 and 11 is 19. Both Bai Yun and Gao Gao could live 19 more years.

SHI SHI ENJOYS ROLLING IN PILES OF PINE SHAVINGS.

Hua Mei and Mei Sheng have different fathers. Hua Mei's father is Shi Shi, who was born in the wild but injured in a fight with another male panda. Even though veterinarians at the reserve took care of him, he had been too badly hurt to go back to the wild. After spending seven years in San Diego, Shi Shi returned to China in 2003 and now lives at the Wolong Nature Reserve.

Mei Sheng's father is Gao Gao (pronounced GOW GOW). He too was born in the wild and was rescued by villagers after nearly two-thirds of his right ear had been torn away in a fight. He was released into the wild after several months of treatment, but he kept going back to the reserve and the people who had cared for him. Finally he was allowed to stay. He arrived at the San Diego Zoo after a long plane journey early in 2003.

ONE HUNDRED DAYS OLD

AUGUST 1999						
SU	MO	TU	WE	TH	FR	SA
1	2	3	4	5	6	7
8	9	10	11	12	13	14
15	16	17	18	19	20	21
22	23	24	25	26	27	28
29	30	31				

SEPTEMBER 1999						
SU	MO	TU	WE	TH	FR	SA
			1	2	3	4
5	6	7	8	9	10	11
12	13	14	15	16	17	18
19	20	21	22	23	24	25
26	27	28	29	30		

OCTOBER 1999						
SU	MO	TU	WE	TH	FR	SA
					1	2
3	4	5	6	7	8	9
10	11	12	13	14	15	16
17	18	19	20	21	22	23
24	25	26	27	28	29	30
31						

NOVEMBER 1999						
SU	MO	TU	WE	TH	FR	SA
	1	2	3	4	5	6
7	8	9	10	11	12	13
14	15	16	17	18	19	20
21	22	23	24	25	26	27
28	29	30				

Some Chinese people believe it is bad luck to name a baby before it is 100 days old. So the panda cubs born at the San Diego Zoo were given names after they were 100 days old. The female cub, Hua Mei, was born on August 21, 1999. You can use a calendar to count out 100 days. Start counting on August 22, when she was one day old. Stop counting on day 100. Hua Mei was 100 days old on November 29. The name Hua Mei means "China-U.S.A." and "splendid beauty."

AUGUST	21	NOVEMBER	29
	−2		−2
AUGUST	19	NOVEMBER	27

The male cub, Mei Sheng, was born on August 19, 2003. There is an easy way to figure out when he was 100 days old. He was born 2 days earlier in August than Hua Mei, so all you need to do is count back—or subtract—2 days from November 29. By changing both the start and end date by the same amount, the difference remains the same. Mei Sheng was 100 days old on November 27. Mei Sheng's name means "born in the U.S.A." and can also mean "beautiful life."

"CAN I TRY SOME, TOO?"

Lights. Camera. Pandemonium! Mei Sheng made his public debut with his mom when he was four months old. Crowds of people waited in long lines to catch a glimpse of the baby panda. A keeper carried Mei Sheng from his den to an outdoor exhibit area and placed him in the wooden box that was like another den. The exhibit had a climbing structure made of logs, a tall elm tree, and logs on the ground for climbing practice. A moat separated the panda yard from the viewing area.

Whenever it rained, Bai Yun would squeeze into the back of the box so she wouldn't get wet. Mei Sheng would be pushed to the front, where raindrops fell on him. He didn't mind a bit. A panda's fur is so thick that it's like a raincoat.

POO'S CLUES

MEI SHENG MUNCHES SOME BAMBOO.

Bai Yun's keepers weigh her poop each day to see how much of the nutrition in the bamboo she's eaten has been absorbed. Twice a day they collect her poop to weigh it. They might find 24 piles of panda poop overnight but only 7 piles during the day.

To find out how much more she poops at night, subtract 7 from 24. One way to do this is to change the numbers so the subtraction problem is easier. The number 10 is a friendly number. To get 10, add 3 to 7. But you must also add 3 to 24. When you add the same amount to both numbers, the difference between them stays the same.

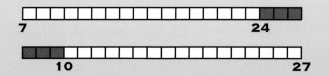

Adding 3 to 24 gives us 27. Now we can subtract our friendly 10 to get 17. The difference between 27 and 10 is 17. The difference between 24 and 7 is also 17.

```
24 NIGHTTIME POOPS + 3 →  27  (ADD 3 TO BOTH NUMBERS)
− 7 DAYTIME POOPS   + 3 → −10  (SUBTRACT OUR FRIENDLY 10)
                          ───
                          17   MORE PILES OF POOP AT NIGHT
```

Bai Yun has 17 more poops at night.

OOPS! LEARNING TO CLIMB IS TOUGH.

At about five months, Mei Sheng became very playful during his weekly exams. To keep him from biting his keepers and the doctors, he was given things to play with, such as a piece of bamboo or a plastic bucket.

Mei Sheng also liked to play with his mother. One day as they played near the moat, the cub got too close to the edge. Down into the moat he tumbled! His mother went right down to get him. Soon, though, the cub learned to climb out of the moat on his own. He was starting to climb trees, too, but when he tried to walk on a tree limb he would often flip underneath and plop to the ground. He didn't give up. He'd climb right back up and try again.

BEDTIME FOR PANDAS

HUA MEI RESTS ON HER CLIMBING STRUCTURE
WHEN SHE IS SIX MONTHS OLD. MEI SHENG
LIKES TO SLEEP IN THE SAME SPOT.

At six months, Mei Sheng slept about 16 hours a day. To find out how many hours he was awake, subtract 16 from 24 hours, the number of hours in a day. To make a friendlier number to subtract, add 4 to 16 to get 20. To keep the same difference between the numbers, you must add 4 to 24, which is 28.

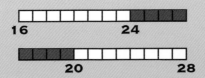

Now the subtraction is easy. Subtract 20 from 28 and the difference is 8.

```
 24  HOURS IN A DAY  + 4 →  28 (ADD 4 TO BOTH NUMBERS)
–16  HOURS ASLEEP    + 4 → –20 (SUBTRACT OUR FRIENDLY 20)
────────────────────────────────────────────────────────
                            8 HOURS AWAKE
```

Mei Sheng was awake 8 hours a day.

MEI SHENG SITS ON HIS FAVORITE PERCH.

Hua Mei made her public debut when she was six months old. It wasn't long before she clawed her way up on the climbing structure and slept on a thick branch.

Mei Sheng often chose the same place to sleep. And when he woke up, he was always ready to play. If his mother was on the ground sleeping on her belly, he would climb onto her back, biting her fur and her ears until she woke up. Sometimes he'd race off to climb a small pine tree. One day he fell out of the tree and bounced into the moat. Fortunately pandas have such thick fur that they don't get hurt when they fall. Moments later he bounded out of the moat and climbed the same pine tree again.

POUNDS OF PANDA

SENIOR KEEPER DALLAS RIPSKY WEIGHS HUA MEI.

At four months, Hua Mei weighed 15 pounds. By the time she was seven months old she weighed 30 pounds. How much weight had she gained in three months?

To make a friendly number to subtract, add 5 to 15 to get 20. To keep the same difference between the numbers, you must also add 5 to 30 to get 35.

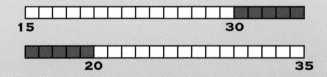

Subtract 20 from 35 and the difference is 15. So Hua Mei gained 15 pounds in three months.

30 POUNDS AT 7 MONTHS + 5 → 35 (ADD 5 TO BOTH NUMBERS)
–15 POUNDS AT 4 MONTHS + 5 → –20 (SUBTRACT OUR FRIENDLY 20)
_____
15 POUNDS GAINED

Another way to figure this out is to think about doubles. When you double 15, you get 30 (15 + 15 = 30), so that means 15 subtracted from 30 is 15.

"NO ONE CAN GET ME UP HERE!"

When Hua Mei was seven months old, she spent most days and nights up in a tree. Her mother would grab her with both paws and pull and pull, trying to get her down, but would finally give up. For about two weeks, Hua Mei didn't leave the outdoor exhibit.

At the same age, Mei Sheng often spent most of the day sleeping in an elm tree, thirty feet above the ground. The San Diego Zoo staff wrapped metal sheets around the upper tree branches to keep him from climbing too high, but the cub climbed right around them. In the wild a panda cub will stay in a tree while his mother is away searching for bamboo to eat. High in a tree, a panda cub is safe from predators.

HAPPY BIRTHDAY, HUA MEI!

At one year, Hua Mei weighed about 59 pounds. By the time she celebrated her third birthday, she had reached her adult weight of 200 pounds. To find out how much she had grown in two years, subtract 59 pounds from 200 pounds.

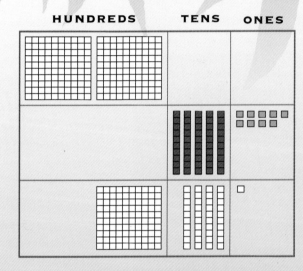

HUNDREDS **TENS** **ONES**

200 POUNDS ADULT WEIGHT

−59 POUNDS WEIGHT AT ONE YEAR

141 POUNDS GAINED IN TWO YEARS

One way to figure this out is to subtract each place value. Normally you would start by subtracting hundreds, but since there aren't any hundreds to subtract, begin by subtracting tens, then ones.

First subtract 50 from 200, which is 150. Then subtract 9 from 150. Since 10 is a friendlier number than 9, subtract 10 from 150 to get 140. Then add 1 back to get 141, because you subtracted 1 too many.

200 − 50 = 150 (SUBTRACT 5 TENS)

150 − 9 = ? (SUBTRACT 9 ONES, BUT IF THAT'S TOO HARD . . .)

150 − 10 = 140 (. . . SUBTRACT 10 BECAUSE IT'S A FRIENDLY NUMBER)

140 + 1 = 141 (THEN ADD 1 BACK)

So Hua Mei gained 141 pounds in two years.

BIRTHDAY PARTIES CAN WEAR A GIRL OUT!

BAI YUN HELPS HUA MEI EAT HER BIRTHDAY ICE CAKE.

For her first birthday, Hua Mei was given an ice cake with a stick of bamboo as a candle. Bai Yun was by her cub's side, helping her eat her birthday cake, which had carrots and yams and bamboo frozen inside. Now that Hua Mei had most of her teeth, she could eat crunchy foods.

On her third birthday, Hua Mei received three different birthday cakes. One of the cakes had a panda face that used eggplant for the black parts. First Hua Mei bit off the ears, then she placed the cake on her belly and rolled around with it. She took turns eating and playing with the cake until it finally melted. Mei Sheng will have a party and special cakes for all of his birthdays at the San Diego Zoo, too.

TROUBLE FOR PANDAS

HUA MEI DANCES FROM BRANCH TO BRANCH.

The panda census, or population count, released in 2004 indicates that there may be as few as 1,600 pandas left in the wild. Pandas are in trouble because their habitat is disappearing. Wild pandas live in forests scattered across six mountain ranges in central China. In 1988 the panda habitat was 5,000 square miles. But in 2004 it was only 700 square miles.

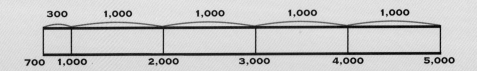

300 + 1,000 + 1,000 + 1,000 + 1,000 = 4,300 SQUARE MILES

One way to figure out how many square miles of habitat were lost is to use a method called **adding up.** Start at 700. Adding 300 gets you to 1,000, which is a friendly number to work with. Then add 1,000 four times until you get to 5,000. To the original number, 700, you have now added a total of 4,300. This is how many square miles of habitat pandas have lost. Chinese and American scientists are working together to find ways to save and expand the forests where pandas live.

28

HUA MEI AND HER MOTHER SPEND ONE OF THEIR LAST DAYS TOGETHER BEFORE THEY ARE SEPARATED.

At eighteen months, Hua Mei was separated from her mother for longer and longer periods of time. She didn't seem to mind living by herself. Pandas are solitary animals, and it is normal for young pandas to leave their mothers when they are eighteen to twenty months of age. Early in 2004, Hua Mei left the San Diego Zoo and now lives at the Wolong Giant Panda Conservation Center in China.

When Mei Sheng is three years old, he will also leave San Diego. But the San Diego Zoo will continue working with Chinese scientists to study giant pandas and to help increase their numbers. Hua Mei and Mei Sheng have drawn worldwide attention to pandas and the problems they face. These two famous cubs, and all panda babies yet to come, represent hope for the future of pandas.

"HOW DO I GET DOWN?"
MEI SHENG PRACTICES CLIMBING.

HUA MEI FINDS THE PERFECT PERCH.

MEI SHENG SNUGGLES WITH HIS MOTHER.